GARTH BROOKS

A Real-Life Reader Biography

Phelan Powell

Mitchell Lane Publishers, Inc.
P.O. Box 619 • Bear, Delaware 19701

Second Printing

Real-Life Reader Biographies

Selena	Robert Rodriguez	Mariah Carey	Rafael Palmeiro
Tommy Nuñez	Trent Dimas	Cristina Saralegui	Andres Galarraga
Oscar De La Hoya	Gloria Estefan	Jimmy Smits	Mary Joe Fernandez
Cesar Chavez	Chuck Norris	Sinbad	Paula Abdul
Vanessa Williams	Celine Dion	Mia Hamm	Sammy Sosa
Brandy	Michelle Kwan	Rosie O'Donnell	Shania Twain
Garth Brooks	Jeff Gordon	Mark McGwire	Salma Hayek
Sheila E.	Hollywood Hogan	Ricky Martin	Britney Spears
Arnold Schwarzenegger	Jennifer Lopez	Kobe Bryant	Derek Jeter
Steve Jobs	Sandra Bullock	Julia Roberts	Robin Williams
Jennifer Love Hewitt	Keri Russell	Sarah Michelle Gellar	Liv Tyler
Melissa Joan Hart	Drew Barrymore	Alicia Silverstone	Katie Holmes
Winona Ryder	Alyssa Milano	Enrique Iglesias	Freddie Prinze, Jr.
Christina Aguilera			

Library of Congress Cataloging-in-Publication Data
Powell, Phelan.
    Garth Brooks/Phelan Powell.
        p. cm. — (A real-life reader biography)
    Discography: p.
    Includes index.
    Summary: Examines the life and work of the popular singer-songwriter whose early struggles led to overwhelming success.
    ISBN 1-58415-004-1
    1. Brooks, Garth Juvenile literature. 2. Country musicians—United States Biography Juvenile literature. [1. Brooks, Garth. 2. Musicians. 3. Country music.] I. Title. II. Series.
ML3930.B855P68 1999
782.421642'092—dc21
[B]
                                                                              99-10093
                                                                                      CIP

ABOUT THE AUTHOR: Phelan Powell is a freelance writer who has written several books for young adults. Her titles include biographies of John Candy, Tom Cruise, John LeClair, and Hanson (Chelsea House) and Jeff Gordon (Mitchell Lane). A former newspaper reporter, Phelan lives just outside Philadelphia, PA with her husband and two sons.

PHOTO CREDITS: cover: Globe Photos; p. 4 AP Photo; p. 8 David Rossman/Shooting Star; p. 12 Archive Photos; p. 14, 28 Ron Davis/Shooting Star; p. 22 Paul Fenton/Shooting Star; p. 29 Mike Segar/Archive Photos; p. 30 AP Photo/Elaine Thompson.

ACKNOWLEDGMENTS: The following story has been thoroughly researched, and to the best of our knowledge, represents a true story. Though we try to authorize every biography that we publish, for various reasons, this is not always possible. This story is neither authorized nor endorsed by Garth Brooks.

Table of Contents

Chapter 1
"You Got a Deal!"

Garth Brooks knew he wanted to make music his life ever since, as a youngster, he would play the comb when his family got together for some music time at home. In 1985, when he was 23 years old, he went to Nashville, the home of country music. Although he was sent away without any hope of a music contract, he decided to try again in 1988.

He was with his friend Bob Doyle, a music publisher who owned Major Bob Music. Doyle was impressed by Garth's talent as a guitarist and music writer and had signed him on in 1987. Doyle brought

Garth Brooks loved music all his life.

Garth to The Bluebird Café, where many famous country singers started out. Doyle wanted Garth to see and hear other promising performers onstage. Garth knew there were a lot of important people in the audience, executives from music companies who were looking for fresh, exciting talent to sign.

One of those executives was a man named Lynn Shults, who worked for Capitol Records. A few weeks before The Bluebird Café show, Garth had gone to Shults' office and played for him. Shults told Garth he was not interested in signing up the hopeful singer.

But something happened that night that changed Garth Brooks' life forever. Garth was not just to be a member of the audience that night. For some reason, several acts did not show up. To fill one of those empty spots, Garth was called from the audience to play a couple of songs. He played two. At the end of his short set, Lynn Shults came running up

Garth went to The Bluebird Café to hear other promising performers onstage.

excitedly to Garth and Bob Doyle and started pumping Garth's hand.

"You got a deal!" he exclaimed to Garth. Shults wanted to sign him to a Capitol Records contract immediately. Garth wondered out loud what had changed Shults' mind after the man had turned him down just a short time before. Shults admitted he was overwhelmed at the way Garth could relate to his audience as he spilled out his heart with his songs. It was obvious to Shults that Garth had what it took to make those listening to him become part of the experience of his songs. The top people at record companies know that is the key quality to selling a singer and his music.

Within a month, Garth signed a contract with Capitol Records, who now believed they had a new success story in the making. They gave Garth $10,000 up front, which showed they believed in his future. That was more money than Garth had ever seen in his life. But within a few years, that

Garth was called from the audience to play a couple of songs. After hearing him play, Capitol Records wanted to sign him immediately.

Garth Brooks is driven to be the best he can be in his field. He is a lively entertainer. Here he performs to a sold-out crowd at Copps Coliseum in Ontario, Canada in September 1996.

$10,000 would seem like lunch money compared to the millions of dollars he would eventually make as a famous singer. His dream had come true beyond his wildest imaginings.

It seemed to Garth as if it had taken a long time to get to this point, to finally be recognized by the people who count the most for a performer, the executives of the big music companies. But as Garth later said, looking back on his success, "Sometimes things that last forever, take forever."

Garth Brooks is driven to be the best he can be in his field, and he has always worked hard at it. As he says, "Never relax, never take that breath, never stop to get that drink of water. You know you can always smell roses when you're running with them in your hand. Keep your focus on the music!"

"Some—times things that last for—ever, take forever," said Garth.

Chapter 2
A Musical Family

Garth's mother, Colleen Carroll Brooks, was a singer.

Troyal Garth Brooks was born on February 7, 1962, in Tulsa, Oklahoma. Oklahoma is a big oil producing state, and Garth's father, whose first name is also Troyal, worked as a draftsman and engineer for an oil company. Garth's mother, Colleen Carroll Brooks, was a singer. She sang on radio and television shows and had even been under contract with Capitol Records in the mid-1950s. She recorded four singles for them.

It was a second marriage for Troyal and Colleen when they came together. The marriage brought four children immediately into the household, and then the couple had two more children together: Kelly, then Garth. The parents did not believe in making a distinction between their children and stepchildren, so they made it clear that they were all one family and would act like one.

When Garth was just a youngster, his family moved to the small town of Yukon, Oklahoma, which became Garth's hometown. The town today proclaims the famous singer as their own, and they proudly display a billboard saying so.

Understandably, having six kids in the house made for a busy time, so eventually Colleen gave up her singing career to take care of the children.

Young Garth had a good relationship with both his parents. "My dad was a cool guy. He pretty much cut straight to it. And Mom could make the worst things sound great. They were a great pair, because

When Garth was a young— ster, his family moved to Yukon, Oklahoma.

they'd level each other out. One was an extreme realist, one was an extreme dreamer. And both were extreme doers."

Early on, Troyal became Garth's hero. "If I could be like any man in the world, it would be him," he says of his father.

Garth's childhood was a happy one, because his parents not only loved and supported each child, but they would make special and fun occasions of each holiday. Kids were always coming over to the Brookses' house, where they were made to feel wanted and accepted. Once a week, a special night was set aside for what the Brookses called Funny Night. Everyone in the family participated, with Garth's

Garth (left) with his parents, Colleen and Troyal Brooks

brothers, Jim, Mike, Jerry, and Kelly, and his sister, Betsy, playing instruments such as the harmonica and guitar and, for young Garth, the comb. Music was not the only way to show their talents on these nights. Sometimes they did little skits or performed imitations of people that they had practiced.

"Garth would want to be right in the middle of it," Betsy remembers, "and he'd capture your attention."

Unlike many children whose first experiences of music are tedious piano lessons and lonely hours of practicing by themselves, Garth saw, through his family's delight in performing, that music was fun.

Many new types of music and performers emerged during the early years of Garth's life, and he found himself drawn to a lot of different sounds. As a teenager, his tastes in music ranged from Kiss and Queen to country stars George Jones and Merle Haggard to musicians somewhere in between rock and country. It was not

It was not until he was out of high school that Garth decided to follow the country music path.

until he was out of high school that he decided he wanted to follow the country music path.

At Yukon High School, Garth gave his best to his athletic interests. He played a wide variety of sports, including running track and playing baseball, basketball, and football. Garth was an active quarterback on the Yukon Millers team for three years. He was later made a defensive lineman. By the end of his high-school years, he knew an earlier dream he had cherished, which was to be a

Garth has enjoyed baseball all his life. He participates in various charity baseball games.

professional athlete, would not come true for him. However, he never could have guessed that years later, his music fame would allow him to mingle in professional baseball.

Garth had done very well in his studies at Yukon High, and now it was time to give college a try.

Chapter 3
Oklahoma State University

Garth Brooks applied to nearby Oklahoma State University, where his older brother, Kelly, was already a sophomore. The happiest part of Garth's college experience was that he and Kelly became roommates. They were only 18 months apart in age and got along really well.

Garth decided to try something new in college: javelin throwing. An ancient sport, javelin throwing required him to have a strong arm. Because he had developed his arm playing sports in high school, he was pretty good with the javelin. He also ran track for the four years he was at

In college, Garth continued to pursue athletics.

OSU. But once again, his performance was not good enough for him to consider becoming a professional.

Meanwhile, Garth played his guitar. Eventually, instead of just playing for his fellow students, Garth began playing at local hangouts in the college town of Stillwater. He became popular enough that some of the places began paying him for his music. Sometimes he would earn $100 for playing for only four hours. He was not rich, but already he had become a professional musician. Garth would play and sing songs by popular artists of the day or country music songs such as those by one of his personal heroes, George Strait.

His musical life was becoming a passion, but it was not paying all the bills. He had to take other jobs, one of which was as a bouncer in a bar. His job was to take care of people who got out of hand and might start a fight. He would either calm the person down or ask them to leave (bounce them out). This job, even though it

His athletic perform– ance was never good enough for him to consider becoming a profes– sional.

seems fairly routine, proved to change Garth's life. One fight he had to break up was between two women. When Garth helped one of the women home, he liked her so much that he asked her for a date. She was a student at Oklahoma State University, and her name was Sandy Mahl.

Sandy remembers that when they were dating, Garth would often play at a place called Wild Willie's Saloon. "He'd just get up and he would play anything from Neil Young to Willie Nelson, Elton John, Billy Joel, or Dan Fogelberg. It was whatever anyone could yell out. He'd say, 'I don't really know that one but I'll try it.' And you would have guys saying, 'No, it's this verse next,' and they'd come up and sing along with him on the mike."

By the time Garth graduated from college in 1984, he was playing six nights a week in local bars. He had studied advertising in college, but all he wanted to do was play music. Garth was still dating Sandy, but his

Eventually, Garth's music became his passion. But, it did not pay all the bills.

dream of making it big in country music forced him to make a decision. It was time to go to the place where his dreams could come true: Nashville, Tennessee.

Chapter 4
Nashville

Garth Brooks believed in himself and his ability to succeed so much that in 1985 he took off for Nashville without hesitation. "I thought you'd go there, flip open your guitar case, play a song, and someone would hand you a million bucks," he remembers.

He had an overpowering need to let the world hear his songs, or even the songs of others sung in his own special way. "Your songs are your swords, your power. It's amazing the size of the sword you carry. I'm looking for beliefs that need to be

> **He had an overpowering need to let the world hear his songs.**

stated in this day and time. I try to let people know that they aren't working for nothing, that what they see when they close their eyes at night doesn't always have to be a dream."

Garth's first trip to Nashville, though, turned out to be a nightmare. The city is full of record companies, but it is difficult to get invited into one of their offices. When Garth finally got a chance to talk to an executive at the American Society of Composers, Authors and Publishers (ASCAP), the man flatly sent him away. He had no interest in the young starry-eyed artist who stood eagerly before him.

Garth was crushed. He didn't even have the courage to go back to Stillwater and OSU—and particularly to Sandy. He did not want her to see him as a failure. He went home to Yukon and stayed with his family for a while. This helped him regain enough strength to return to Stillwater and let his friends, including Sandy, know what had

Garth's first trip to Nashville turned out to be a nightmare.

happened to his great dream. His Nashville failure did not make Sandy any less fond of Garth, however. In fact, a few months later, on May 24, 1986, Garth and Sandy got married.

For a while Garth worked in a sporting goods store and played with a band at night. In 1987, he led a band called Santa Fe, which played locally as well as in surrounding states. Garth thought they were good enough to go to Nashville and make it big. The band stuck together for several months in Nashville, but they figured they just were not going to get the record contract they came for. When the band broke up, Garth and Sandy stayed in the big city. Once again, Garth went knocking on record company doors, trying to sell himself and his music.

Garth remembers that time as one of the most difficult of his life. "I thought we weren't going to make it. I thought we were going to crash, trash out, go into debt, poverty and stuff. It had nothing to do with music.

For a while, Garth worked in a sporting goods store and played with a band at night.

It was two people, newly married, struggling against debt. I thought it was over."

At one point Garth told Sandy that it would probably be better for them to forget his dream and just go back to Oklahoma. Sandy refused to let Garth let himself down. "I think you're good enough and you think you're good enough, so we're going to stay right here," she told him.

The young couple stayed. Finally, on a night in 1988 when he went to The Bluebird Café to watch what some

Garth with wife, Sandy

would have called his competition, Garth got his break.

Garth has his own ideas about what competition is: "I think competition makes things better. I think competition makes the music better. I think it makes film better. So the greatest competition I think there is, is the competition within yourself. Just being the best person you can be. It's cool, too, because yourself is just brutally honest. There's just things you can't hide from yourself because you know yourself too well."

That night, Garth bested his competition when Capitol Records told him they wanted him. Within ten months, Garth's first album, called *Garth Brooks*, was in the record stores. It sold more than 6 million copies, which made it the best-selling country album of the 1980s. In order to go on tour and help sell the album, Garth put a band together. He called it Stillwater.

"There's just things you can't hide from yourself because you know yourself too well."

Chapter 5
The Thrill Ride

In 1989, Garth received three nominations at the Academy of Country Music Awards.

Like a ride on an old roller-coaster, the initial Stillwater tour started out slow and steady. In many places, Garth Brooks was not yet known to the fans of country music. Many of his audiences were small and quiet. But that did not last long. Enthusiasm for Garth's album spread across the country. *Garth Brooks* quickly ranked number two on the Billboard Country Music chart.

In the spring of 1989, the dreamer who never stopped working toward his dream found himself at the Academy of Country Music Awards. Garth received three nominations. He did not win, but he felt honored to be part of such an important music ceremony. The roller-coaster had topped its first big hill and has been going full speed ever since.

Millions of people across the country came to know Garth when he released his first music video, called "The Dance." Added to the concerts he gave, the video helped him reach many fans with his music.

Garth has never considered his songs as simply songs. "Whether I write them or whether I sing someone else's, usually nine times out of ten it's going to be a message," he has said. "You get three minutes to tell the world somethin', punch right through the chest, grab their heart, and say, 'Listen!'"

Shortly after Garth made his second album, called *No Fences*, his first album reached more than a million copies sold. He started receiving numerous country music awards; he toured London, England;

Millions of people across the country came to know Garth when he released his first video, called "The Dance."

and he appeared on *The Tonight Show.* In 1992, Garth was asked to perform at the American Music Awards in Los Angeles, California. He was chosen as the Country Male Artist of the Year; his song "The Thunder Rolls" was chosen Country Single of the Year; and *No Fences* was chosen Country Album of the Year.

In 1992, Sandy and Garth's first child was born.

In the face of such honors, however, his mind was not totally focused on receiving the unbelievable admiration of such a huge number of people that night. He was thinking of Sandy, who was pregnant with their first child. Taylor Mayne Pearl Brooks was born to Garth and Sandy on July 8, 1992. Now that they were three, and the threat of poverty had faded away, Sandy and Garth bought a huge home in Goodlettsville, Tennessee, which is just outside of Nashville.

When Garth made a Christmas album at the end of 1992, he donated some of the proceeds to the Feed the Children charity. Like most big-hearted, successful people, Garth realized the virtues of sharing some of his good fortune. In 1993 he sang at Super Bowl XXVII. His picture was soon on the cover of all sorts of national magazines, from *Time* to *The Saturday Evening Post* to *People*.

Garth had worked hard through his life to make his dream come true, and, thanks to Sandy's encouragement, he never gave up. "I think sometimes you gotta put yourself to the test," he says. "You've gotta get in waters where you know it's not a sure win, 'cause that's where some of the most brutal losses come; and it really hurts, but the wins are even better out there. And that's what I say to anybody: Don't play it safe. Hang it out there on the edge and see what happens."

Within five years, Garth had six albums out, and two more, collections of his best songs, were released in 1994. Profits from the first best-of album were given to the Ronald McDonald Children's Charities.

When Garth made a Christmas album at the end of 1992, he donated some of the proceeds to the Feed the Children charity.

The thrill of selling 60 million albums by 1994 was second only to the birth of Sandy and Garth's second child on May 3, 1994. It was another girl, and they named her August Anna.

Garth and Sandy with their daughter, August Anna.

Garth and his band found millions of fans outside the United States when they went on a tour of 13 countries. In 1996 Garth won Country Male Artist of the Year, Overall Artist of the Year, and Country Album of the Year awards at the American Music Awards. At the end of 1998, he broke a music industry record by selling more than one million copies of an album (*Garth Brooks Double Live*) in one week. Shortly after that, the same album was number one on the Billboard Top 200 Chart.

In February 1999, the San Diego Padres announced that Garth Brooks had been invited to spring training on a non-roster basis. Instead of paying him a salary, the Padres donated $200,000 to Garth's new baseball-related Touch 'Em All Foundation, which he created to benefit children's charities. Even though he was playing in the minor leagues, his agreement with the Padres allowed him to fulfill a dream he had abandoned years before: to be a professional athlete. One at a time, with some talent, hard work, and a little luck, Garth Brooks is making all his dreams come true.

But all this success has not kept Garth from relating to his fans. He sets a limit on the amount

Garth (right) sings alongside one of his band members at the opening of his free concert in New York's Central Park, August 7, 1997.

of money that can be charged for tickets to his concerts so that as many fans as possible can have the chance to see him perform. And he has always felt a personal responsibility for the words that he sings.

"I feel country music is taking on a new role, taking on responsibility. We have to consider what we sing, because more and more people are listening to country music, and kids are listening to it earlier. We have a chance to shape society, in a way," Garth says.

"If God came down here with the box that had the reason for living in it, I'd like to find just two words—*the music*. That would be neat."

In 1999, Garth was a non-roster invitee to the San Diego Padres spring training in Peoria, Arizona.

Discography

Garth Brooks (1989)
No Fences (1990)
Ropin' the Wind (1991)
Beyond the Season (1992)
The Chase (1992)
In Pieces (1993)
The Garth Brooks Collection (1994)
The Hits (1994)
Fresh Horses (1995)
Sevens (1997)
Double Live (1998)

Chronology

- Born on February 7, 1962, in Tulsa, Oklahoma, to Troyal and Colleen Brooks
- Graduates from Oklahoma State University in Stillwater in 1984
- Begins performing professionally at local bars in Stillwater, Oklahoma
- Goes to Nashville in 1985 but fails to win a music contract
- Marries Sandy Mahl on May 24, 1986
- Signs with Major Bob Music, a music publishing company, in 1987
- Signs with Capitol Records in June 1988
- Forms his band, Stillwater, in 1989
- Brother Kelly joins Garth to be his business manager; sister Betsy joins Stillwater as a guitarist and backup singer
- In 1990, Garth is inducted into the Grand Ole Opry
- First child, Taylor Mayne Pearl, is born July 8, 1992
- In 1993, Garth receives Entertainer of the Year Award for the third time
- Second child, August Anna, is born May 3, 1994
- Tours throughout the world 1996–1998 to packed houses
- Receives Favorite Male Musical Performer in 1997 at People's Choice Awards
- November 1998, *Garth Brooks Double Live* album sells more than a million copies in one week and hits number one spot on Billboard Top 200 Chart
- 1999, invited to Spring training with the San Diego Padres

Index